Jack London's

Wolf House

Gregory W. Hayes and J. Matt Atkinson

Illustrations by Steven Chais

Valley of the Moon Natural History Association
2400 London Ranch Road
Glen Ellen, California 95442
www.jacklondonpark.com
E-mail: jlondon1876@gmail.com
Telephone: (707) 938-5216

Printed in the United States of America

in memoriam

I. Milo Shepard

Foreword

WOLF HOUSE —
A Dream Almost Come True

I am building my dream-house on my dream-ranch.
My house will be standing, act of God permitting, for a thousand years.

—*Jack London*

In the first decade of the twentieth century, California writer Jack London and his wife, Charmian, dreamed of building and living in the perfect residence. In "Wolf House" they envisioned what they hoped would become their ancestral home, a refuge, workshop, and place of celebration, all under one roof—after an impoverished, itinerant childhood, the only true home Jack London would ever call his own. The author of *Call of the Wild*, famous for his northland tales of men and women striving against the elements, had grown up on the Oakland waterfront, traveled the world and hoped to escape the rat race of city life by sinking down roots in the pristine Sonoma Valley.

Construction on his "dream-house" began in 1911, five years after the catastrophic San Francisco earthquake and firestorm. Working closely with San Francisco architect Albert Farr, the Londons settled on a rustic design that included fireproof materials such as local volcanic rock and unpeeled redwood logs mounted on a concrete foundation that could hold a "40-story building." The 15,000-square-foot house rose four stories, commanding a view of the Sonoma Valley, contained twenty-six rooms and nine fireplaces, and cost between $40,000 and $75,000 (in 1913 dollars). It was to include the latest in modern conveniences, such as hot water, electric heating and lighting, and refrigerating and vacuum cleaning plants.

Wolf House got its name from Jack's nickname—London, who had become famous by writing about wolves, was called "Wolf" by poet friend George Sterling. Tragically, only a month before the Londons were to move in, on August 22, 1913, fire destroyed the home. "It was a very quick fire," said a devastated London. "The walls are standing, and I shall rebuild." But already suffering from poor health, London never recovered from the blow—his dream ended in nightmare. Three years later, at the age of forty he died of kidney failure, his reconstruction plans never realized.

From that time on, the ruins of London's dream house have been a beacon for London followers from all over the world, attracting them even before the property became a state park open to the public in 1960.

Although both Londons were avid photographers, because of the timing of the unexpected fire, very few photographs were taken of the nearly completed house. Collected here in book form for the first time are the best of the snapshots that were taken, along with facsimiles of the most significant and informative documents regarding the Wolf House. They have been culled from the Jack London archives at the author's home in Glen Ellen, at the state park established in his honor, as well as from the Huntington, Bancroft, and Oakland libraries. In addition, the authors of this book have augmented the primary historical photographs and drawings with present-day computer-generated graphics.

Perhaps most intriguing for readers will be the reprints of words written by the Wolf House's authors, Jack and Charmian London, as well as their contemporaries about what the home and its loss meant to them—Jack's startling (albeit rhetorical) promise to burn it down himself if it didn't live up to his expectations. For the detail-oriented and the conspiracy theorists, there are painstaking enhancements of the original blueprints and the never-before published findings of the 1995 academic forensic study done on the origins of the mysterious fire that prevented the Londons' dream from coming true. Ω

Following architect Farr's rendering, this computer-generated illustration recreates a bird's eye view of Wolf House from the southeast.

Acknowledgments

This book could not have been created without the support of the Valley of the Moon Natural History Association, a non-profit educational group of dedicated state park volunteers which financed its research and publication. We would also like to give special thanks to Steven Chais who answered our prayers for help in a realm we knew nothing about, for his unflagging enthusiasm in working on this project with us, and for his countless hours of close inspection, keyboarding and skillful computer-driven re-visualization that produced the informative illustrations that appear throughout these pages and help to breathe life into what was an often overwhelming array of antique black-and-white images. Credit is also due to California State Parks, especially to Jack London State Historic Park and its unit rangers Sheryl Lawton and Deej Beane and curator Carol Dodge for providing access to the archival collection and to the Wolf House ruins to allow the necessary measurements, original photographs, and copies of historic photographs to be made, and for the state's permission to publish them as well.

We are grateful to I. Milo Shepard, executor of the Trust of Irving Shepard, and Sara S. Hodson, Curator of Literary Manuscripts at the Henry E. Huntington Library in San Marino, California, for granting access to their London collection and permission to reproduce photographs and notes from the author's correspondence. Thanks also go to Special Collections librarian Dayle Reilly and Dean Barbara Butler for opening to us the Waring Jones Reading Room and London research collection at Sonoma State University's Jean and Charles Schulz Information Center. The Bancroft Library at the University of California, Berkeley, and what remains of the California History room at the main downtown branch of the Oakland Public Library (where a young Jack London matriculated, briefly, and got his start in reading literature, respectively) were generous in sharing their considerable resources.

We are indebted to Dr. Robert Anderson of San Jose State University for allowing ours to be the first print publication to incorporate his forensic team's fascinating arson investigation report. Many people went to a lot of trouble to help us track down scarce Wolf House images and references: Connie Johnson and Homer Haughey; Jeanne Campbell Reesman; the late Russ and Winnie Kingman, bless them, and their Jack London Foundation; and pilot and aerial photographer extraordinaire Robert Campbell of Chamois Moon. For permission to reprint their ninety-three-year old eyewitness dispatches gratitude is owed to *The Press-Democrat, Santa Rosa*. And to Jane Merryman, copy editor and longtime librarian at the state park, we are grateful for sorting through and weeding out our careless mistakes. Ω

Contents

Introduction

Jack and Charmian London

Tue Aug 19, 1913
$300.00 in bank . . .

Penning brief notes in her diary, Charmian London captured the details of what she and husband Jack London described as the "Bad Year." In 1913 the famous writer and his wife were beset by a variety of reversals of fortune: Charmian was still recuperating from a physically and emotionally difficult miscarriage, and Jack was told of a serious kidney ailment after having an appendectomy. Both needed rest and relaxation, but their dream house—Wolf House—was rising, soaking up much of their time, energy, and money, as they strove to finish and move into the mansion by October 1.

In Wolf House, the Londons envisioned their ideal home. In it, he wrote, "Utility and beauty must be indissolubly wedded. Construction and decoration must be one."

Physical work on the house began in April, 1911. But as early as summer, 1906, after buying 129 acres referred to as the old "Greenlaw place," London had workers building a Swiss chalet-style stone and wooden barn, landscaping the house site, and planting fruit trees, vines and hedges. On April 18 of that year the devastating San Francisco earthquake and subsequent firestorm found the Londons in residence at Wake Robin Lodge in Glen Ellen. The quake leveled much of Santa Rosa, fifteen miles to the northwest; on the London acres it toppled a shoddily built hollow stone wall of his new barn. "The walls were lies," London wrote of them in disgust. "They were beautiful, but they were not useful." He vowed not to repeat mistakes learned from disasters, natural or otherwise: "Act of God permitting," he said, "my house will be standing for a thousand years." Toward this end, working closely with architect Albert Farr and master stonemason Natale Forni, London insured that the design included a massive concrete foundation slab and fireproof materials such as volcanic rock and redwood pillars still clad in their fire-retardant bark.

By late August of 1913 it was time to make plans for moving in. Although their expenses were mounting, the Londons hoped to weather the Bad Year and regroup in their new home. Along with other new ranch buildings going up, and hand in hand with Jack London's dream of fertile acres for his farm, the busy couple also had expectations of raising a family in the ancestral home. For her part, once settled in, and after resetting her emotional compass by sailing on the bay, Charmian London was going to attempt to become pregnant again, despite the potential danger. On Tuesday, August 19, she wrote in her diary:

> *$300.00 in bank and big obligations coming. But the concrete silo is wonderful as it rises, and the corn is going in soon.*

The next day she wrote:

Pleasant days—happy, lucky. Practicing a lot, sewing pretties and "flimsies," moving, absorbed a great deal in Wolf House. I tell mate, 6 weeks on water, then I'll try again. All sorts of rooms for the nursery.

There is no entry for August 21, but local records show that a heat wave, with temperatures higher than common in the Sonoma Valley in summer, held sway over the region. Then, on Friday, August 22, Charmian wrote:

At midnight Eliza comes to tell us of fire. And our Wolf House is destroyed.

Mate and I are cheerful enough until we get back, at about 5 am. Mate breaks down completely.

*Sat Aug 23, 1913
100 degrees
Little sleep. Feel horribly shaken—heart seems jumping out of my body, and tears are terribly near the surface. Our dear, dreamed-of home.*

*Sun Aug 24, 1913
Such dreams! Sleep and wake, sleep and wake.*

In evening we get Forni to supper and jolly him up. He's almost crazy. "My child! My child!" he cried, before the burning house.

Ω

Chalet-style barn built by London before Wolf House was begun.

PART 1—The Building

Seated on 3rd floor railing of nearly completed Wolf House (southeast corner),
Jack London reviews blueprints.

The House Beautiful
By Jack London[1]

And now to my own house beautiful, which I shall build some seven to ten years from now. I have a few general ideas about it. It must be honest in construction, material, and appearance. If any feature of it, despite my efforts, shall tell lies, I shall remove that feature. Utility and beauty must be indissolubly wedded. Construction and decoration must be one. If the particular details keep true to these general ideas, all will be well.

I have not thought of many details. But here are a few. Take the bath-room, for instance. It shall be as beautiful as any room in the house, just as it will be as useful. The chance is, that it will be the most expensive room in the house. Upon that we are resolved—even if we are compelled to build it first, and live in a tent till we can get more money to go on with the rest of the house. In the bath-room no delights of the bath shall be lacking. Also, a large part of the expensiveness will be due to the use of material that will make it easy to keep the bath-room clean and in order. Why should a servant toil unduly that my body may be clean? On the other hand, the honesty of my own flesh, and the square dealing I give it, are more important than all the admiration of my friends for expensive decoration schemes and magnificent trivialities. More delightful to me is a body that sings than a stately and costly grand staircase built for show. Not that I like grand staircases less, but that I like bath-rooms more.

I often regret that I was born in this particular period of the world. In the matter of servants, how I wish I were living in the golden future of the world, where there will be no servants—naught but service of love. But in the meantime, living here and now, being practical, understanding the rationality and the necessity of the division of labor, I accept servants. But such acceptance does not justify me in lack of consideration for them. In my house beautiful, their rooms shall not be dens and holes. And on this score I foresee a fight with the architect. They

[1] Excerpted from *Revolution and Other Essays*, Macmillan, 1909.

shall have bath-rooms, toilet conveniences, and comforts for their leisure time and human life—if I have to work Sundays to pay for it. Even under the division of labor I recognize that no man has a right to servants who will not treat them as humans compounded of the same clay as himself, with similar bundles of nerves and desires, contradictions, irritabilities, and lovablenesses. Heaven in the drawing-room and hell in the kitchen is not the atmosphere for a growing child to breathe—nor an adult either. One of the great and selfish objections to chattel slavery was the effect on the masters themselves.

And because of the foregoing, one chief aim in the building of my house beautiful will be to have a house that will require the minimum of trouble and work to keep clean and orderly. It will be no spick and span and polished house, with an immaculateness that testifies to the tragedy of drudge. I live in California where the days are warm. I'd prefer that the servants had three hours to go swimming (or hammocking) than be compelled to spend those three hours in keeping the house spick and span. Therefore it devolves upon me to build a house that can be kept clean and orderly without the need of those three hours.

There will be hardwood floors in my house beautiful. But these floors will not be polished mirrors nor skating-rinks. They will be just plain and common hardwood floors. Beautiful carpets are not beautiful to the mind that knows they are filled with germs and bacilli. They are no more beautiful than the hectic flush of fever or the silvery skin of leprosy. Besides, carpets enslave. A thing that enslaves is a monster, and monsters are not beautiful.

The fireplaces of my house will be many and large. Small fires and cold weather mean hermetically sealed rooms and jealous cherishing of heated and filth-laden air. With large fireplaces and generous heat, some windows may

London's perch is generated by a computer using the photograph on opposite page to illustrate the varied look of stone and wood materials.

be open all the time, and without hard-
ship all the windows can be opened
every little while and the rooms flushed
with clean pure air. I have nearly died
in the stagnant, rotten air of other people's houses—especially in the Eastern
states. In Maine I have slept in a room
with storm-windows immovable, and
with one small pane, five inches by six,
that could be opened. Did I say slept?
I panted with my mouth in the opening
and blasphemed till I ruined all my
chances of heaven.

For countless thousands of years
my ancestors have lived and died and
drawn all their breaths in the open air.
It is only recently that we have begun
to live in houses. The change is a hard-
ship, especially on the lungs. I've only
got one pair of lungs, and I haven't the
address of any repair-shop. Wherefore
I stick by the open air as much as possible. For this reason my house will
have large verandas, and, near to the
kitchen, there will be a veranda dining-
room. Also, there will be a veranda
fireplace, where we can breathe fresh
air and be comfortable when the eve-
nings are touched with frost.

I have a plan for my own bedroom.
I spend long hours in bed, reading,
studying, and working. I have tried
sleeping in the open, but the lamp at-
tracts all the creeping, crawling, butt-
ing, flying, fluttering things to the pages
of my book, into my ears and blankets,
and down the back of my neck. So my
bedroom shall be indoors.

But it will not be of indoors. Three
sides of it will be open. The fourth side
will divide it from the rest of the house.
The three sides will be screened against
the creeping, fluttering things, but not
against the good fresh air and all the
breezes that blow. For protection
against storm, to keep out the driving
rain, there will be a sliding glass, so
made that when not in use it will oc-

10

"The Courtyard" of "Residence for Mr. Jack London,
Glen Ellen, California" (called "Wulfruh"), first envisioned and rendered by Architect Albert Farr.

"The Hall looking towards Steinway. Albert Farr, Architect, San Francisco." Charmian's grand piano was to hav
its own alcove in the two-story living room ("Hall").

Architect Albert Farr's sketch of Wolf House before construction.

cupy small space and shut out very little air.

There is little more to say about this house I am to build seven to ten years from now. There is plenty of time in which to work up all the details in accord with the general principles I have laid down. It will be a usable house and a beautiful house, wherein the aesthetic guest can find comfort for his eyes as well as for his body. It will be a happy house—or else I'll burn it down. It will be a house of air and sunshine and laughter. These three cannot be divorced. Laughter without air and sunshine becomes morbid, decadent, demoniac. I have in me a thousand generations. Laughter that is decadent is not good for these thousand generations.

—*Glen Ellen, California, July, 1906*

Ω

London beside massive volcanic stones dynamited at local quarry and used in construction.

11

Letters from Jack London

Looking up to living room level from "stag party" room in basement.

Dear Greek:

For over a year now... I have been planning this home proposition, and I am now just beginning to see my way clear to it. I am really going to throw out an anchor so big and so heavy that all hell could never get it up again. In fact, it's going to be a prodigious, ponderous sort of an anchor.

[to poet and friend George Sterling, May 28, 1905]

Dear Mr. Phillips:

Will you consider this story? [*The Valley of the Moon*] As regards the reason for making this request, let me explain: It is very simple. I am building my dream-house on my dream-ranch. I want the building to go on, and at the same time I want to stop my short story stunt for awhile and write a novel that I have close to heart. This is such a novel. As regards rate of payment, suppose we say 12 ½ cents a word?

[to Roland Phillips, editor at Cosmopolitan Magazine, *May 30, 1911]*

Dear Woman:

The stone house grows. Two four-horse wagons hauling lumber today—20 loads of it. Bar accidents, we'll be in our own home next fall.

[to Charmian, November 16, 1912]

Dear Mr. Scott:

In order that you may not think me a wastrel, I enclose herewith a very inaccurate article upon the home I am building. I expect to move into this home the coming fall. To put the tile roof on the house will cost $2500.00 itself, and I have just closed contract to that

The west wing—containing kitchen, dining room, piano alcove, library and London's workroom—awaits Spanish roof tiles.

effect. Of course, this has nothing to do with other material in the house, nor with my stone masons, plumbers and carpenters wage lists. Also, I have just bought another 500 acres and added it to the ranch. Also, I am remodeling and reconstructing all the farm buildings, and workmen's houses, on the ranch. Also, I am going ahead with my regular planting of eucalyptus trees. And, finally, the half of the house which is already completed is all paid for. I pay for my work and for my material month by month as it goes along.

[to Frank Scott, Century Co., December 21, 1912]

Dear Brett:

First, the house: Some eight or nine years ago I bought the land on which our house-site is situated. Some six or seven years ago I planted the house orchard, the house vineyard and the hedges around the house-site. These have been growing ever since. Two years ago I started to build the house. By working very hard and very expensively this summer, we hope to be into the house this fall, not later than October 1. When I tell you that all these years we have been without a house; that I have been without space sufficient to shelve all my books, and that we have waited nine years for the completion of our house to approach, you will see that we have been very patient. As regards my library, it has been mostly stored away in boxes in the various barns on the ranch. Yet these books were my tools and are my tools. Most frequently, when I desire a reference, and look over my limited shelves, I find that the books which I need are stored away in some of the barns.

[to London's publisher George Brett at Macmillan Publishing Co., March 1, 1913]

Dear Brett:

And by October, or the middle or end of October, I hope to be moved over into the new house. Said house goes on apace, and I am well proud of it; but my! it does cost money. But when it is done, I shall be really comfortable for the first time in my life. And I have been pretty patient with the building of that house—not rushing matters in the slightest. Nine years ago I bought the land and picked the house site; so I surely have not shown any undue haste in the matter of housebuilding.

[July 29, 1913]

Unidentified guests admire courtyard and pool. The young redwood stand towering above the house was not used in construction.

Foreman Natale Forni
(1871–1948)

*M*aster stonemason Natale Forni, a native of Spezia, Italy, and builder of several stone structures in Santa Rosa, was hired by Jack London to build Wolf House. London biographer Russ Kingman collected the following notes detailing Forni's recollections of the project:[2]

When he started work there were about 30 men. Rocks [quarried from] across valley. Logs from his own ranch. In summer workers lived in tents—about 8 of them. At night up on hill with jug of wine and ac-

cordion. Jack often came and sang with them. "He was so kind to everybody." Never came on the job without a smile.

[Wolf House] built to last forever. Copper for roof gutters and flashing. And lead in pipes. More cement, less lime, to make house strong. Wire brushed rocks and watered every week. Kept walls wet constantly. No. 1 lumber. 2 floors between each stage for deadening. Some places 3 floors. Inside walls solid timber. Outside logs bolted into inside studs for double security. Forni learned craft in Spezia [Italy] from father.

Were rubbing varnish preparing his living quarters, almost ready to move in. Rags were left in a corner and ignited by spontaneous combustion.

The night the house burned down they all cried (workmen) like children to think of all that good work being wasted.

On night of fire Forni had driven by at 11. About 2 Jack had tears in his eye. Liza [Eliza London Shepard] wept. Everybody stayed all night. He said to Forni, "We'll clean it out and build all over."

After fire [Jack] wasn't the same man no more. Big change came over him.

Kingman recorded the following information from the Londons' diaries:

November 28, 1910	Ride to Boccas to look at rocks. Plan to lay foundation soon.
December 31, 1910	Big redwoods coming down for house.
March 14, 1911	Farr laying out house site – porte-cochère.
March 17, 1911	Jack hires Eliza to oversee house building at $50 a month.
May 9, 1911	To Boccas to see them quarry their own rock.
September 21, 1911	Wolf House growing. Tank finished.
October 3, 1911	Stone pillars for arches around patio at Wolf House are growing wonderfully.

---

[2] From the collection of the Jack London Foundation, Glen Ellen, California.

After two years of intensive labor, in 1913 the Wolf House was nearing completion.

Stonemason Natale Forni's keystoned arcades of volcanic rock lining the reflection pool (pictured today as part of the preserved ruins) were reminiscent to some of a courtyard in the Alhambra in Granada, Spain.

Ranch Superintendent
Eliza London Shepard

(1867–1939)

"House—Big House—My! it looks great. The teams are busy with scrapers digging out the space for the last foundation wall by the redwoods—and everybody and everybody who has seen the walls already up—men who know—material men—coming for orders—workmen & etc.—say they are simply splendid."

[Eliza, from a letter to her brother, June 2, 1911]

Eliza, Jack London's stepsister, was eight years his senior. A direct beneficiary of her supervision when she helped their father John London raise the children in the family, Jack had come to depend on his big sister early in his life. Knowing how organized and reliable she was he hired her in 1910 to oversee all the ranching activities on his Glen Ellen farm. Many notes mentioning construction details indicate that he left much of the nuts and bolts work of directing the complicated house-building project to her as well. According to Charmian, Eliza was "scarred to the soul" by the loss of Wolf House. After her brother's death, she remained on the 1400-acre spread helping Charmian convert it into a guest ranch during the Great Depression.

When she died in 1939 her ashes were laid to rest near "the stone that the builders rejected," on the knoll not far from the Wolf House ruins, alongside the ashes of her brother Jack. Ω

A portion of London's 1400-acre Beauty Ranch. The 2463-foot peak of Sonoma Mountain is at top left. Wolf House site is marked at lower right, in yellow circle.

Visitors on balcony overlooking pool circa 1913, while house was nearing end of construction.

A recent picture of the ruins shows laundry room and servants' quarters located in this southeast basement room.

Architect Albert Farr
(1871–1947)

Albert Farr of San Francisco

Born in Nebraska and raised in Yokohama, Japan, and a California resident from 1890, architect Albert Farr of San Francisco designed the famous Wolf House for his friend Jack London. As boys, London and Farr may have first met while living in East Oakland, where they were next-door neighbors.[3] Farr and other well-known architects such as Julia Morgan and Ernest Maybeck helped popularize the Arts and Crafts–style home in California.

In the Bay Area neighborhoods of Pacific Heights, Belvedere, and Piedmont, Farr created rustic brown shingle-sided houses (many of them still inhabited). Some of the earliest reinforced concrete buildings in San Francisco and one of the earliest reinforced concrete bridges, at 40th and Piedmont Avenue in Oakland, were drawn by Farr's pen. He also designed the Benbow Inn in Garberville (1926) and in 1923 the residence at 2570 Jackson Street in San Francisco that currently houses the French Consul-General. Ω

[3] From communication with I. Milo Shepard, October 21, 2007, Glen Ellen, California.

Farr's original sketch of the Benbow Inn near Garberville, California, on the Eel River.

Albert Farr, Architect
    Foxcroft Building,
        San Francisco.
                - LIST OF MATERIAL. -

4 pc. 16-inch   logs   Bark 6 ft. long Posts in Balcony
11 pc. 12-inch   "   "   6 "   Mullions
3 pc. 16-inch   "   "   7 "   Lintels
5 pc. 16-inch   "   "   20 "   Trusses
2 pc. 16-inch   "   "   28 "   "
10 pc. 12-inch   "   "   12 "   "
10 pc. 12-inch   "   "   6 "   "
8 pc. 16-inch   "   "   16 "   Posts in living
                                            room and hall

25 pc. 16-inch   "   "   7 "   Stairs
40 pc. 6-inch logs   Bark 8 ft. long Beams over arcade
10 pc. 6-inch   "   " 10   "   "   " porch
8 pc. 8-inch   "   " 14   "   "   " loggia
200 lin.ft. 12-inch logs, bark on to cut 20 ft. lengths,
                                 Beams over Pergola.
1700 "   " Small poles about 1-ft.long & 2 inches dia Pergola
 400 "   "   6-inch diameter for Purlins
 250 "   "   24-inch logs to be squared up for lintels
24 pc. 6-inch logs Bark 14 ft.long   - Pergola rafters
15 pc. 6-inch   "   "   12 ft.long   "   "
220 " 6-inch   "   "   6 ft.long   Rafter ends
 20 " 10-inch   "   "   18 ft.long   Verge Boards
 40 " 8-inch   "   "   4 ft.long   Lookouts in Gables

SAVE ALL EXTRA STRAIGHT BRANCHES, etc., as they may be useful.

Farr left behind artifacts such as the working blueprints found in the appendix of
this publication as well as the materials list shown here.

Today, visitors first glimpse the ruins from the side, through bay, madrone and redwoods trees.

Modern bracing supports walls of two-story living room and "stag party" room.

Entry breezeway (with water tower at far end).

View approaching front of ruins from old Hill Road (porte cochère was to the right).

Below is the same view, during construction.

Bricks are stockpiled in preparation for the creation of nine fireplaces (in six chimneys). London's wood frame sleeping tower (top, center) was the only room on the fourth floor.

Raising the Wolf House: a digital view

First a foundation strong enough to support a 40-story building and the tank for the pool were constructed, then the stone walls were raised rock by rock before the bark-covered timbers were added. London planned for Wolf House to withstand earthquakes and fires.

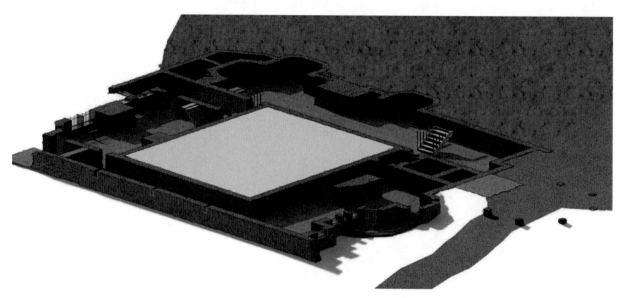

Southeast view—Central block marks placement of architect Farr's arcade, courtyard, and "reflection pool" tank that was deepened by the Londons to provide an actual swimming pool.

Southeast view at later stage—Structure was visually dominated by stonework but lightened by numerous windows.

dwood timbers and wood paneling completed the upper levels, tying together the three wings of the house.

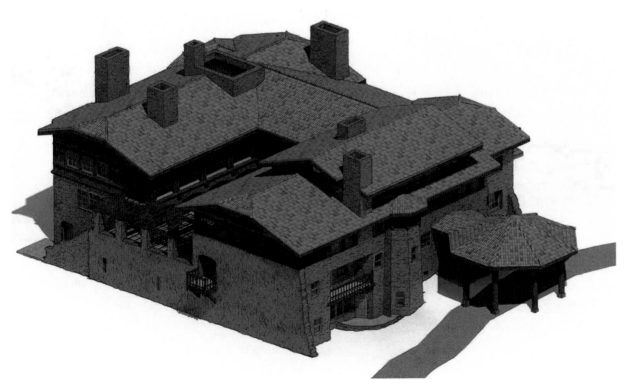

A red ceramic tile roof capped the structure. The nine fireplaces were intended to provide natural heat, the built-in water tower to charge the plumbing by gravity-flow.

Architectural design software technology has enabled modern viewers to see the Wolf House imagined from all angles in its pre-fire configuration.

A Description of Wolf House
George Wharton James[4]

If in the building of a home the builders should express themselves, then Jack and Charmian London are building one of the most individualistic homes in the world. It is located on the London ranch in the Sonoma Valley—the valley of the moon, as the poetic Indian name suggests. Since his first land purchase he has bought two or three adjoining ranches, until now the estate comprises about twelve hundred acres. Of this, nearly eight hundred acres are wild hillside and four hundred are under cultivation. With a glorious outlook on all four sides over fertile fields, with woods and mountain slopes, the house is being built on a knoll, with a most picturesque clump of redwoods at the back. Being out-of-door people, fond of water, the home is built around a patio, in the center of which is a water pool or tank of solid concrete forty by fifteen feet and six feet deep, fed by water from a cold mountain spring, and in which black bass will be kept, and where one may occasionally take a plunge—if he is brave and hardy enough.

Weeks have been spent upon the concrete bed which is practically the foundation of the house. Mr. London has here carried out an idea of his own, viz., that in an earthquake country as California, a house designed to be permanent should be especially guarded in its foundation. He reasons that a house built on a gigantic slab of concrete will move as a unit, and not one wall incline in one direction when the quake occurs. Anyhow the architect has supervised the putting in of a bed

[4] From "A Study of Jack London in His Prime," *Overland Monthly*, May, 1917, vol. LXVIII, no. 5.

of concrete sufficiently deep, thick and strong to sustain a forty-story skyscraper on a sandy foundation.

The architect is Mr. Albert Farr of San Francisco, a man of knowledge, experience and imagination, and as soon as Mr. and Mrs. London laid before him their ideas, he went to work to materialize them. The house is built chiefly of five materials, all of which are local products—redwood trees, a deep chocolate-maroon volcanic rock, blue slate, boulders and concrete. The London ranch furnishes the redwoods which are to be used with their jackets on, the rough deep-red colored bark harmonizing perfectly with the rough rock of the foundation. The rock is used exactly as blasted. It is not quarried in the sense of being worked regularly. It is simply blasted out and some chunks weigh several hundred pounds, some merely a few pounds and some as much as a ton or more. Just as they come they are hauled and placed in appropriate places.

The result is immensely effective and attractive. The first floor is already built so that the effect is definitely known, and can be properly estimated. The house is U shaped, the main portion being eighty-six feet wide, with two eighty-two feet wings. The concrete water tank occupies the center of the patio, or open court. Around the tank will be a five-foot strip of garden, and this is the only piece of formal or conventional flower garden on the estate. Balconies built of redwood trunks are to surround the court.

The steps leading to the second story and the second story itself are to be built of the great boulders or cobble stones found on the estate, also the outside chimneys, and a builder has been found whose artistic work in the handling of these boulders is a joy and a delight.

The rough tree trunks will form the architectural lines of the porte-cochère, pergolas and porches, while the rafters

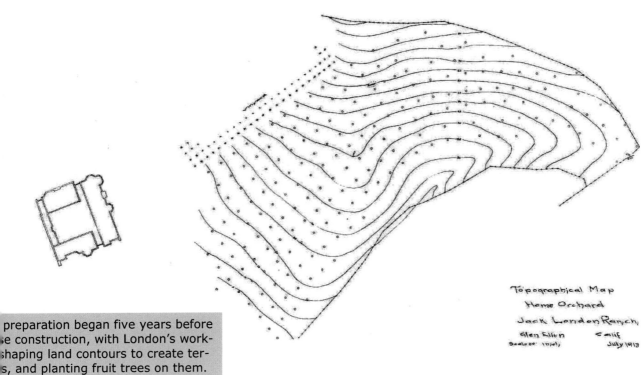

Topographical Map
Home Orchard
Jack London Ranch,
Glen Ellen   Calif
Scale 50' (inch)   July 1913

preparation began five years before
e construction, with London's work-
shaping land contours to create ter-
s, and planting fruit trees on them.

25

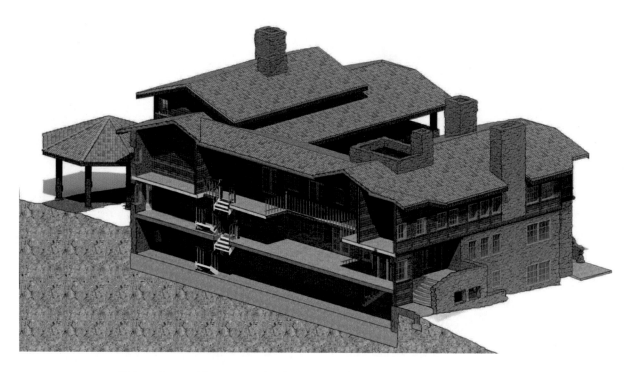

This cutaway illustrates the locations of interior walls and stairways.

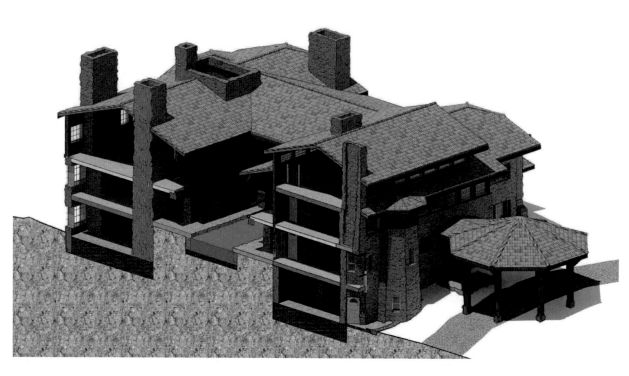

Cross-section through courtyard

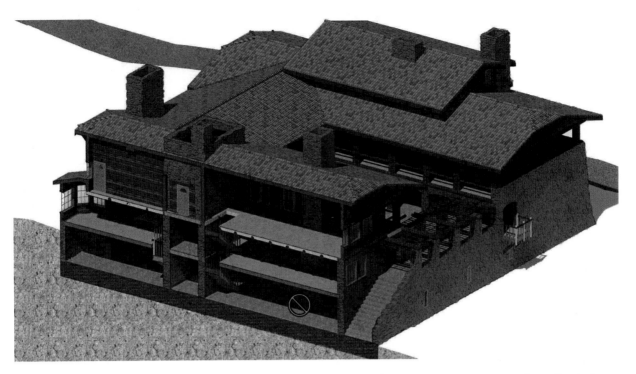

West wing contained London's library and workroom above basement dining room, where fire is believed to have had its origin (red circle).

Imagined view across the courtyard from the pergola toward the breezeway and living room.

Actual construction photograph of courtyard view of Wolf House pool and breezeway.

are to be hewn out of rough redwood logs and kept in the natural finish. A charming effect is to be obtained by interlacing the tree trunks in the gables and balconies with fruit tree twigs. The roof will be of Spanish tile, colored to harmonize with the maroon of the rock and the redwood.

The interior is to be finished after the same rustic and individualistic fashion. It is to be essentially a home for the two people who are building it—a workshop for Mr. London, a home for Mrs. London, and a place where they can gather and entertain their friends. Hence these three ideas have been kept distinctly in the foreground. Mr. London's workroom is on the second floor, and is to be a magnificent room, nineteen by forty feet, with the library, exactly the same size, directly underneath, and the two connected with a spiral staircase. These two rooms are entirely apart from the rest of the house, thus affording perfect seclusion to the author while engaged at his work. His regular habit is to get to writing directly after breakfast, and he never writes less than a thousand words, his regular daily

stunt. If this requires five hours, six, nine or merely two, it is always accomplished, and then the rest of the day is given over to hospitality, recreation or farming.

The chief feature of the house is the great living room, eighteen by fifty-eight feet, and extending over two stories high, with rough redwood balconies extending around the second floor. Open rafters for ceiling and gables, and an immense stone fireplace, which will be fed daily with gigantic logs from the woods on the estate, will give it a cheerful, homelike, though vast and medieval appearance.

The entrance way begins between two gigantic redwoods—and then leads to the porte-cochère, a roomy place big enough for the handling of the largest touring cars.

Immediately from the porte-cochère one enters the large hall, which, except for massive, handsomely wrought iron gates, will be perpetually open, reaching completely from the front to the rear of the building. From this hall three large guest rooms, the patio and the author's workshop are reached on the left hand side, and on the right a reception room, with coat rooms, toilets and all conveniences, a gun-room, the stairs and the large living room. One of the two large alcoves of the living room is to be especially arranged for Mrs. London's Steinway grand piano, a kingly instrument, which gives her intense pleasure, and which will assuredly afford great joy and entertainment to her guests.

Long ago Mr. and Mrs. London fully decided the question that city life had not enough compensation to offer for home life. So they are building with this thought in view—to make a home for themselves where they can welcome and entertain all the friends they desire. They both laugh heartily at the comment of a city lady who, visiting the growing house and not knowing that any one could hear her, exclaimed: "What fools they are! Building such a glorious house where none can see it!" as if the chief end in building a home was for "someone to see it." The Londons have a right appreciation of values, and they know how to place things. The first requirement of a house is that it shall be a home for those who are to live in it—the

appreciation of others is a secondary consideration. From this viewpoint the London house will be ideal.

It is to contain its own hot water, heating, electric lighting, refrigerating, vacuum cleaning and laundry plants—the latter with steam dryer rotary wringer—a milk and store room, root and wine cellar.

Its name is Wolf House, a reminder of London's book plate which is the big face of a wolf dog, and of his first great literary success, "The Call of the Wild."

Ω

The author's book plate

London's sleeping tower and Charmian's quarters on 3rd and 4th floors of east wing overlooked the "Valley of the Moon."

29

PART 2—The Destruction

Charmian's Eyewitness Account[5]

On August 18, with but $300 in bank, and large obligations pressing, [Jack] negotiated another mortgage in order to complete the Wolf House before winter.

Charmian working on her diary.

The Bank placed an insurance on the Hill Ranch covering half the amount loaned. There was no other insurance on the huge purple-red pile, since every one agreed that rock and concrete, massive beams and redwood logs with the bark on, were practically fireproof unless ignited in a dozen places, owing to the quadrangular construction and cement partitions.

Nevertheless, three nights later, August 22, the entire inflammable part of the high stone shell was destroyed. I was awakened by voices from Jack's porch. Tiptoeing out, I saw Eliza, by his bedside, point in the direction of the Wolf House half a mile away, where flames and smoke rose straight into the windless, star-drifted sky.

Teams were harnessed, and leaving the Japanese to keep an eye on things at home, if incendiarism was in the air, we drove leisurely across the ranch. "What's the use of hurry?" Jack demanded. "If that is the Big House burning, nothing can stop it now!"

All the countryside, that had come to feel a personal pride and ownership in "Jack's House," had gathered or was arriving. Public sentiment ran high: and I think, had the criminal or criminals who fired it been detected that night, there would have been a stringing-up to the nearest limbs, in lusty frontier fashion.

Already the beautiful red-tile roof had clattered down inside the glowing walls, and the only care that need be exercised was in regard to the adjacent forest. "Promise me," I said to Jack, so lately out of hospital, "that you won't forget yourself, and overdo." He made the pledge and kept it, very quietly walking about and directing the men.

"Why don't you cry, or get excited, or something, you two?" asked a neighbor. "You don't seem to realize what's happened to you!"

"What's the use?" Jack repeated his thought. "It won't rebuild the house.—Though it can be rebuilt!" he swore cheerfully, purpose in his eye.

Yes, Jack laughed and buoyed up the spirits of the Ranch while his dream castle ascended in lurid smoke that hot August night. But when at four in the dawn, the tension relaxed, and uppermost in his mind loomed the wicked, cruel, senseless destruction of the only home he had ever made for himself, he lay in my pitying arms and shook like a child. After a few moments he stilled, and said:

"It isn't the money loss—though

---

[5] From *The Book of Jack London*, vol.II, Century, 1921.

that is grave enough just at this time. The main hurt comes from the wanton despoiling of so much beauty."

We never did learn whose hand applied the torch. I had all but written "assassin." For the razing of his house killed something in Jack, and he never ceased to feel the tragic inner sense of loss. To this day the ruins of amethystine stone, arch beyond arch, tower above tower, stand mute yet appealing. Total strangers, not all of them women, have wept before them, have cried out, "Poor Jack!"

Forni, the master-mason . . . was like a father who had lost a child, and in danger of losing his reason. Two of his men . . . wandered around the unap-proachably hot ruins like spirits suddenly bereft of Paradise. . . . Even Jack had to turn away when the man who had nailed the last Spanish tile before the conflagration, said with wet eyes: "Well, my roof never leaked, anyway!"

Eliza was scarred to the soul by the sudden wiping out of her work—she had superintended the building from start to finish.

It should be thought of, that house, in relation to Jack, not as a mansion, but as a big cabin, a lofty lodge, a hospitable tepee, where he, simple and generous despite all his baffling intricacy, could stretch himself and beam upon you and me and all the world that gathered by his log fires. Ω

The burnt-out shell of Wolf House.

JACK LONDON'S HOME BURNS

The interior of Jack London's nearly completed new home on his ranch near Glen Ellen was gutted by a fire that started shortly before midnight and which was still burning at 1 o'clock this morning. At that hour the fire was reported to have spread to the wooded hillside and the canyon beyond the new home.

The Londons in the courtyard of the ruins.

A man employed on the London ranch told a Press Democrat representative over the long-distance telephone this morning that the origin of the fire was unknown. At the time he was phoning from the old house at present occupied by Mr. and Mrs. London, he said the novelist and his wife were at the scene of the fire.

The magnificent stone castle on the hillside which Jack London has been building for a long time was nearing completion and the damage done by the fire, of course, was necessarily confined to the expensive woodwork and finish that has been installed, not damaging the walls. The house was to have been ready for occupancy in the fall and a large force of men have been employed on the place.

A telephone message to the Press Democrat from Sonoma this morning also confirmed the news that it was the new London home which the fire destroyed. A fire would do considerable damage to the scenery and wooded hillsides and canyons if it spread to any extent.

At 2:30 this morning Q. R. Wickham, of the Sonoma State Home, telephoned that he had just returned from the scene of the fire and that the entire building had been gutted, leaving nothing but the masonry standing. The fire did not spread to the timber owing to the prompt action of guards on the place when the fire was discovered.

Mr. Wickham said he talked with Mr. and Mrs. London, who had been on the place up to 6 o'clock, and the foreman, who left at 8 o'clock, and none of them had the least idea how the fire originated. The loss will be very heavy.

[*The Press Democrat*, Santa Rosa
August 23, 1913]

JACK LONDON'S CASTLE
IS TO BE REBUILT AT ONCE

View east of Wolf House ruins across Sonoma Valley to Mayacamas mountains.

Damage by Fire Is Estimated Between $30,000 and $40,000

The spirit of Jack London is not depressed by a fire, even if the flames do devastate the interior of a majestic castle he has been building for a couple of years on the hillside on his big ranch near Glen Ellen, occupying the most romantic spot in all the country round. The author of "The Sea Wolf" and other thrilling stories, decreed Saturday that the work of reconstruction of the castle shall commence immediately after the insurance adjuster has inspected the premises. Be it known that Mr. London had $10,000 insurance on the castle, in three companies represented by Luther W. Burris of this city. His loss however, will be between $35,000 and $40,000, according to the estimate furnished on Saturday.

As stated Saturday morning in The Press Democrat's account of the fire, the walls of the castle are still standing, but the interior of the building is gutted. The roof of red tile, which had just been completed, cost $6,000. The marble work, hewn and carved by the experts in that line, until its finish excelled anything like it in this State. This is where the great loss comes in, in addition to the magnificent oak and walnut and the other wood furnishings. As to the origin of the fire, it may have been the work of a disgruntled employee and it may not. Anyhow, it is still a mystery and when the red glow leaped from the turrets of the castle on Friday night shortly before midnight, it surprised everybody who saw it, and particularly surprised Mr. and Mrs. London, who were aroused from their slumbers in their old home some distance away with the news that the castle was burning. It was hard for people here and elsewhere to realize how a fire could do so much damage in a massive stone building and to glance up now it seems harder to imagine with the stout walls and the turreted sides still standing.

[*The Press Democrat, Santa Rosa*
August 24, 1913]

An aerial view of the reinforced ruins as they appear today.

PART 3—The Aftermath

Wolf House ruins today, with water tower in background, pool in foreground.

Letters from Jack London

Dear Joan:

My home, as yet unoccupied, burns down—and I receive no word from you. When you were sick I came to see you. I gave you flowers and canary birds. Now I am sick—and you are silent. My home—one of my dreams—is destroyed. You have no word to say.

[to twelve-year-old daughter Joan,
August 24, 1913]

Gentlemen:

Most satisfactory and gratifying has been the promptness with which your representatives appeared on the scene of my fire, investigated the matter, and settled my claim. So pleasant has our relationship been, that I feel that my catastrophe was almost worth while in order to learn that there was such quick, straight dealing in the world.

[To National Union Fire Insurance Company, August 30, 1913. $6000 policy was issued July 21, 1913. The company used London's note in an advertisement.]

Young redwoods, north side of ruins.

35

Dear Brett:

House was so near ready for occupancy that plumbing, heating, wiring, etc. contracts were completed and I must pay them $10,000. Insurance left me $40,000 net loss.
[to publisher George Brett, September 19, 1913]

Dear Farr:

Now, as I understand the situation, you have carbon copies of contract stipulations and descriptions, and duplicate blue-prints, etc. All these, of course, we shall use to go ahead with when we start to complete the house. As soon as the first frosts come, when the sap is down, I am going to cut the necessary redwood trees again.
[to architect Albert Farr, November 13, 1913]

[To Eliza:]

Get Forni to make our double concrete, fireproof doors for big safe in stone house. It is absolutely necessary for me shortly to get such security for my notes, documents, etc.— some sort of shelving (iron perhaps) must be put in on one side.
[undated note in Jack London's hand]

Eliza:

I am returning . . . Farr's letter and log-list. . . . Now, is this the old, original log-list that Farr first sent us long ago? If so, we won't want the big trees for the porte cochère, since we are to build that in stone. . . . And for heaven's sake, have the men who do the cutting make up lists, accurately describing the different sizes of logs in the various piles, so that all we shall have to do when we come to using them, is to consult the list and haul out what we want.
[to Eliza Shepard, November 26, 1913]

Eliza:

For weeks I've been staring at logs seasoning at stone house, and the more I look at them the more I feel sure there are not enough of them.

Heavens, one put more into the house and on the house before it burned and you will remember my steady insistence that labor cost of handling green logs as against seasoned logs, is a serious matter.

[undated note]

Concrete manuscript vault in basement of Wolf House ruins.

Concrete silos as they appear today after partial restoration in the late 1980s.

Gentlemen:

Here is the situation in a nutshell: I have had what I call a real hard year. . . . I can only tell you that we are going ahead as fast as possible for the rebuilding of the house. Men are chopping down the trees at the present time, which will go into the new house.

[to N. Clark & Sons, December 29, 1913]

London's Cottage

Due to long curing times (a year and half for redwood logs) and other pressing financial matters, Jack London did not get far with rebuilding plans before his death in 1916. From the time of the 1913 Wolf House fire until his death, he placed greater emphasis on building new structures in the heart of the Beauty Ranch where his homely Cottage was located.

London's workers added an extension to his Cottage office so that he could unpack some of his volumes from their rodent-infested storage locations in scattered barns. Just around the corner from his workshop the second of two concrete block silos went up, along with the fabled stone

Construction of London's lake, dam and drain, 1914.

piggery, called the "Pig Palace" by the local press, and the permanent stone dam across the lake, itself an elaborate construction project.

After London's death, Charmian lived on Beauty Ranch for almost another forty years until she passed away in 1955. She stayed in the Cottage and later the museum-like residence she built called the House of Happy Walls half a mile from the Wolf House ruins, writing a biography of her famous husband and compiling photograph scrapbooks, newspaper clippings and correspondence.

Although in her 1921 biography of Jack she indicates her belief that arson was responsible for the Wolf House fire, she seems to have altered her opinion later, as shown in this letter from a Monterey friend who recalled Charmian's words while being shown the ru-

ins sometime during the 1930s:

Charmian pointed to the large mountains back of the impressive ruins. "Zena," she said, "Jack asked me to go horseback riding with him, which we did. He said to me, 'Tomorrow, Mate, we will be in our new home,' but tomorrow never came for us, because the building was burned; whether accidentally or on purpose, who knows? Jack had hired many unskilled laborers to work on the ranch, and it was believed the inside woodwork of the house was rubbed down with inflammable material that caused the fire."

[from Zena Holman to Irving and Mildred Shepard, February 6, 1974]

Origin of the Wolf House Fire

Dr. Robert Anderson's Forensic Group Study[6]

On the night of August 22, 1913, the nearly completed home of author Jack London burned, leaving standing only the three stories–high stone walls and six stark fireplace chimneys. The twenty-six-room home was located in the Valley of the Moon in Glen Ellen, California. The massive lodge of native stone and timber was called Wolf House by London. The home was never rebuilt and the structure was left to stand as it was after the fire. In 1960 the architectural remains and surrounding grounds were passed from the family to the California State Park System. Since 1960 the Jack London State Park has exhibited the structure behind the safety of a fence.

Jack London believed he was building Wolf House to last a thousand years. He had designed steel straps to reinforce the walls against seismic shock. He had treated the wood with the borate preservatives available at the time. He had built a fortress against all attacks except fire. His open design, along with the large use of unfinished timbers and high stone walls allowed any fire, once started, [to] burn rapidly. Many of the windows had not been installed, allowing plenty of air to feed the fire. The thick rock walls that London thought would protect the house actually held in the heat, making the fire hot and swift. Witnesses reported that on their arrival, the entire structure was involved.

.   .   .   .

With the intent to examine the remains of Wolf House for any clues as to the cause of the fire, a multidisciplinary team of ten experts in fire investigation met in Glen Ellen in May 1995 and spent four days going through the remains of what once was a magnificent

[6] Presented January 13, 1996, to the Annual Jack London Birthday Banquet, Sonoma, California.

15,000-square-foot structure.

Pieces of charred wood timbers remaining in the notched masonry pockets where beams connected to the stone walls were studied to determine the most likely progression of the fire. The timbers in the dining room were burnt more severely than in the other rooms. From these clues, the area of origin appeared to be in the dining area located on the ground floor under the library and study. The remaining timbers in the pockets in the adjacent grand living room were canted and showed signs that they had failed first by the force of the tile roof dropping down and then subsequently they were charred by the fire.

The dining room had the only fireplace finished with wood in the house. The eight other fireplaces were finished in stone. The significance appears to be that workmen were applying finishing oils to the wood the day of the fire.

A complete review of the design and construction documents, witnesses' statements, and historical records were considered, along with a computer recreation of the structure in order to determine the most probable cause of the fire.

Although arson cannot be completely ruled out, it is low on the probability list as the dining area would not be the natural choice for an arsonist, nor would an arsonist be content with a single place of origin. In addition, the site was so remote that traveling to the house after dark would have required a lantern (easily observed from the London ranch house) or risked a broken neck.

August 22, 1913 was a typically hot and unstormy California night. This ruled out lightning as a cause.

Building plans showed a telephone system, but there was no evidence that the system had been installed.

The house was wired for electricity as evidenced by electrical junction boxes, conduit embedded in the walls, copper wire, old knob and tube porcelain insulators, and an electrical plan; how-

Surrounding trees made it difficult to protect Wolf House from fire.

ever it does not appear that the system was connected to a generator.

There are several factors that strongly suggest linseed oil-stained rags as being the culprit. There were no furnishings in the house at the time of the fire, yet it was known that the cabinetry was being finished the day of the fire. Even though there are few details of the interior finish, the local Santa Rosa *Press Democrat* newspaper reported that the extent and quality of the walnut and oak interiors were magnificent. We know that Jack's insistence on natural products and natural finishes would demand linseed oil-based stains and varnishes, because these were the "industry standards" for fine woods, as they had been for centuries. The most likely area of origin for the fire has been identified as the kitchen or dining area on the ground floor of the west wing. This and the library

Dining room fireplace was wood-paneled: probable ignition area of fire.

on the floor above would be precisely the areas where these finishes would be used in greatest amounts. The hazards of careless disposal were known to the wood finishers of the age, but knowing of a hazard does not imply elimination of it.

Prior to flaming ignition, the self-heating process of linseed oil on cotton releases large quantities of dense white smoke with a choking, lachrymatory effect, apparently as a result of alkehydes (heaxanal, heptanal, etc.) being generated. This smoke is readily detected by a person in the vicinity or by modern smoke detection systems. In the Wolf House, everyone was gone, and there was obviously no smoke detection system. A loosely piled handful of cotton rags dampened with boiled linseed oil has been shown by our experiments to be capable of self-heating to flaming ignition in a few hours.

The final key is temperature, however. We know that the higher the ambient temperature, the lower the heat losses to the surroundings will be and the faster the oxidation reaction will occur. The one striking observation of London's neighbor was that the night of the fire was the hottest night in memory, thus possibly providing just the one extra factor to enhance ignition. The flaming fire created by even a modest pile of linseed-oiled rags can be sustained as a very energetic fire for more than an hour. This is surely enough heat and time to ensure the ignition of any wooden shelves or cabinetry in close proximity. The time factor is correct. Workmen reportedly left by six pm; Jack may have visited there early in the evening, prior to smoke being detectable. The fire was reported shortly before midnight, which is just the right time frame for carelessly discarded rags to self-heat, ignite, and initiate the tragic fire that hot August night in 1913.

For spontaneous chemical combustion to occur, the presence of an unsaturated oil, such as those derived from linseed, tung, fish, or soybean is required, with sufficient exposure to oxygen and surrounded by enough insulation to allow the exothermic heat of oxidation to accumulate to the point of ignition. Spontaneous combustion can occur in large piles of oily cotton rags, wet with drying oils, such as may accumulate during painting. The combustion starts as a smoldering reaction within the material and propagates slowly outward and eventually bursts into flames.

Computer programs have been used to determine the development of a fire. Using the Hazard I program developed by the Center for Fire Research at the National Institute of Standards and Technology, a time line estimate of the fire was formulated for the origin being in the dining area and is consistent with the report of when the workmen left the site and when the fire was discovered.

The sequence of the fire development was as follows:

- Linseed oil–soaked rags are discarded in the dining room.
- Rags start smoldering and eventually ignite.
- Nearby wood floor ignites and starts smoldering.
- Additional rags and wood floor burst into flame; slow fire growth occurs in room.
- Wood paneling bursts into flame; fire growth rate increases.
- Ceiling temperature reached and flashover occurs.
- Windows break out.
- Fire burns through door to stairway leading to library.
- Fire burns into pantry.
- Fire discovered.

The strong presence of the structure and the man involved left all the team members with a strong feeling of loss that Jack London must have felt. Ω

Wolf House Fire Forensics Team: Robert N. Anderson, Ph.D.; Ralph Crawford; John D. DeHaan, Ph.D.; Michael Mayda; Patrick McGinley; Donald J. Myronuk, Ph.D.; Eleanor Posey, PE; Robert Purington; Marc Rezin; Joseph Zicherman, Ph.D.

The Ruins Enter into Legend

The ruins of Wolf House were designated a California State Historical landmark in 1959 and a National Landmark in 1963. Architectural historians studied the building site and researched its documentation in 1987. They characterized their findings in the Jack London State Historic Park Cultural Resource Inventory, published as part of the state park's General Plan:

Wolf House Significance

The structure was intended by London as his main residence and, as such, is the principal embodiment of the rustic quality that was so large a part of London's self-perception and that pervades all his work at the ranch. In addition, it would have been one of the largest and most elaborate representatives of concepts about informal "natural" living and natural architecture that informed the Arts and Crafts movement, the bungalow building craze, and the vacation architecture of the turn-of-the-century elite. It can be thought of as a combination of one of Greene and Greene's "ultimate bungalows" of southern California and the great lodges of the Adirondack mountains. In many respects, the association with London is secondary. Had it survived, Wolf House would have been one of the most distinguished works of early twentieth-century California architecture.

Ω

42

The grounds around the Wolf House ruins first opened to the public in 1960, after Irving Shepard, Jack London's nephew, gift-deeded the structure to the state of California. A wooden walk-through ramp built by early park custodians afforded visitors complete viewing access to the magnificent structure, but, to discourage wall-climbers, the walkway was removed in 1965 and replaced with the current perimeter fence.

In 1963 KPIX in San Francisco produced the television documentary, *A House is Burning*. As a special effect, 75,000-watt artificial flames and smoke fires were placed throughout the ruins.

Preservationists added steel bracing in 1965 to reinforce the six free-standing chimneys and to help the structure remain in a state of arrested decay.

More so than the nearby London gravesite, the ruins of Wolf House strongly affect visitors from all over the world and from all walks of life. Many claim to feel a spiritual presence while contemplating the rem-

A recent photograph of painted-over graffiti on basement wall of Wolf House, showing the same spot as Winer's "Kirlian" photograph.

nants of London's dream house, and the park log records stories of clandestine nighttime visits that have left behind human funerary ashes and wreaths. In the early 1980s, a professional ghost hunter photographed Wolf House at night with a high voltage "Kirlian" camera. He later returned with a photograph that he claimed showed a spectral Charmian London dressed in a hoop skirt holding two babies, representing a miscarriage and her and Jack's daughter, Joy, who had survived for only one day. Richard Winer, author of *Houses of Terror,* featured the image in his book.

A bracing twenty-minute hike from the parking lot, the ruins are open to the public for viewing daily. On the way down to the Wolf House, a side trail leads up to a pioneer gravesite enclosed by a picket fence. Two children named David and Lillie Greenlaw were buried there in 1876 (Jack's birth year) and 1877. The serene spot was one of the Londons' favorites on the ranch, and Jack had told Charmian, "If I should beat you to it, I wouldn't mind if you laid my ashes on the knoll where the Greenlaw children are buried. And roll over me a red boulder from the ruins of Wolf House."

Three years after his house had burned, Jack London's health failed completely and he died at the age of forty. As he wished, his ashes were laid to rest beneath the Wolf House "stone that the builders rejected."

Ω

The author at work in Glen Ellen.

The Londons' grave stone as it appears now bedecked with moss and ferns.

Appendix — Blueprints and Drawings

Wolf House Ruins   AKB

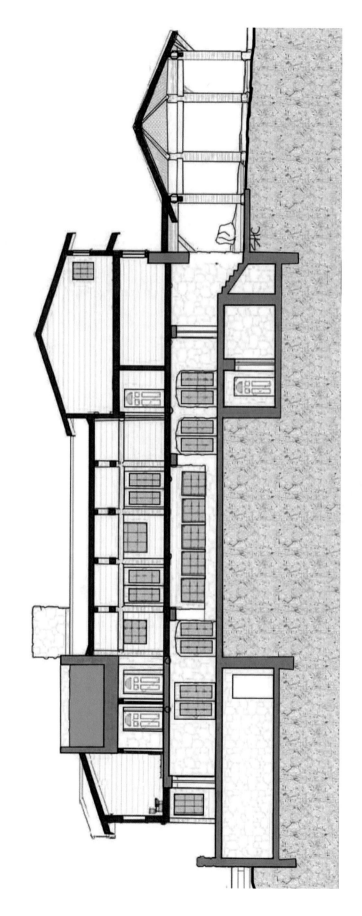

Cross-section shows water tank at upper left, servants quarters in basement at lower right, and dining room at lower left.

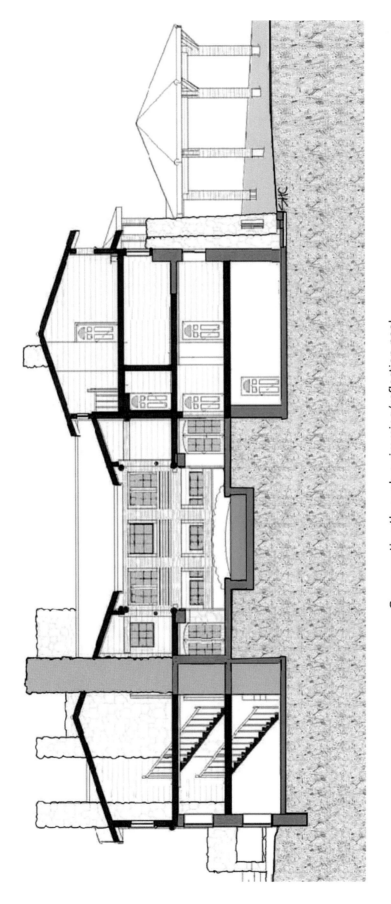

Cross-section through swimming/reflection pool.

47

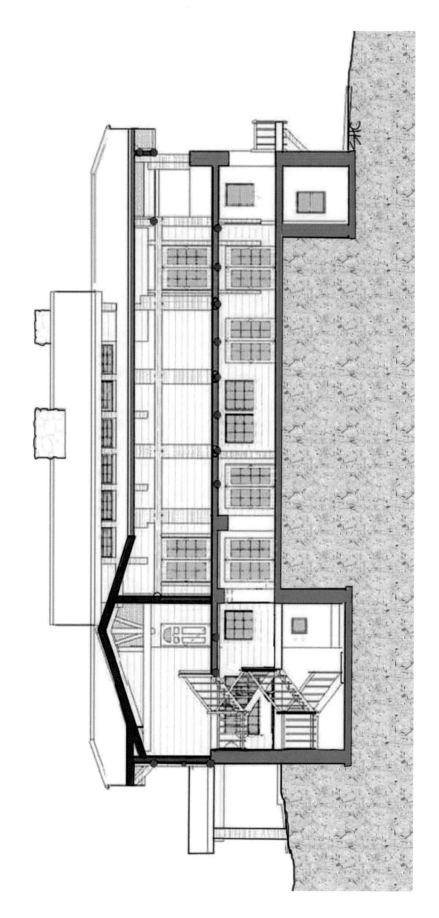

Cross-section shows stairway from Stag party room up through two-story Living room. London's sleeping "tower" is only room on fourth level.

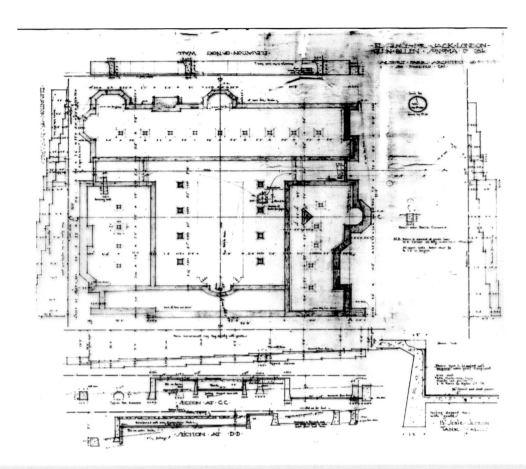

Basement floor plans: Architect Albert Farr's plans are above; computer-generated version is below.

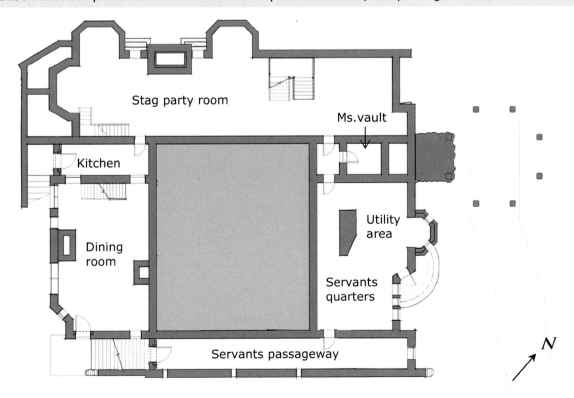

Stag party room

Ms. vault

Kitchen

Utility area

Dining room

Servants quarters

Servants passageway

N

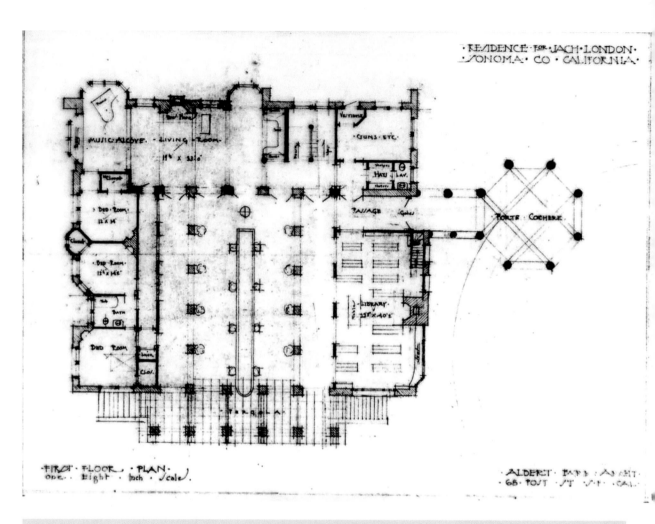

·RESIDENCE·FOR·JACK·LONDON·
·SONOMA·CO·CALIFORNIA·

·FIRST·FLOOR·PLAN·
ONE·Eight·Inch·Scale·

·ALBERT·FARR·ARCH·
·68·POST·ST·S·F·CAL·

First Floor Plans: Farr's plans above show bedrooms in northwest wing and library in southeast wing.
As-built plans below show that order reversed.

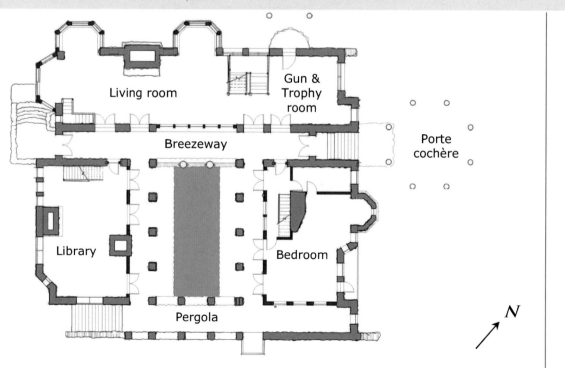

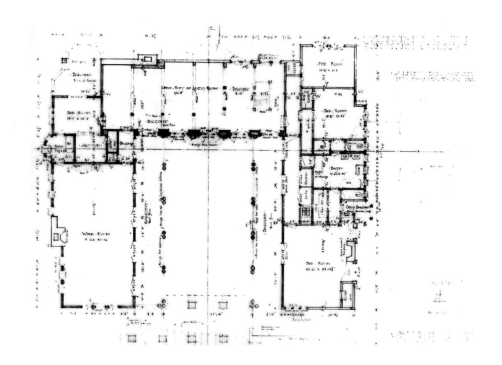

Third Floor Plans: The largest room on this level was the work room in the northwest wing on the left.

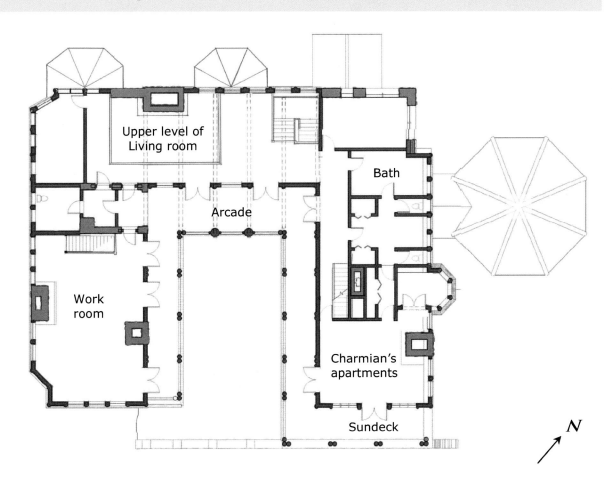

Upper level of Living room

Arcade

Bath

Work room

Charmian's apartments

Sundeck

N

Southeast aerial views

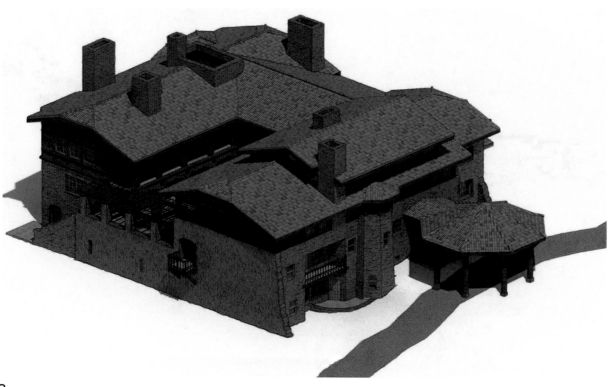

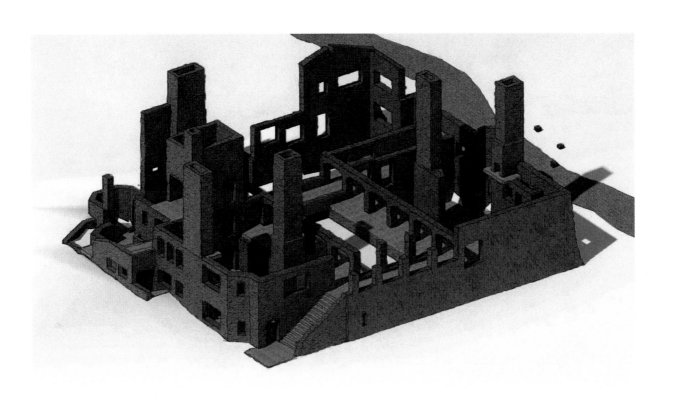

Southwest aerial views

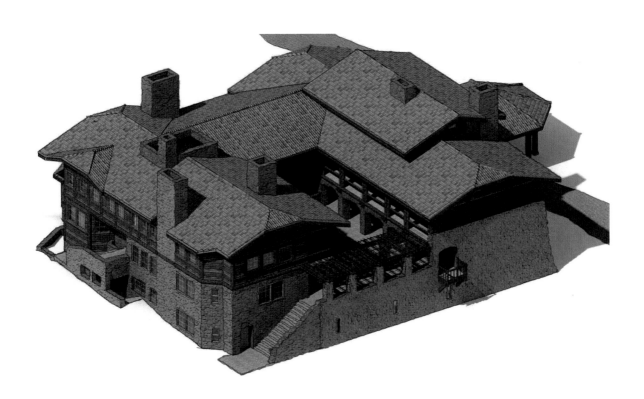

Northeast aerial views

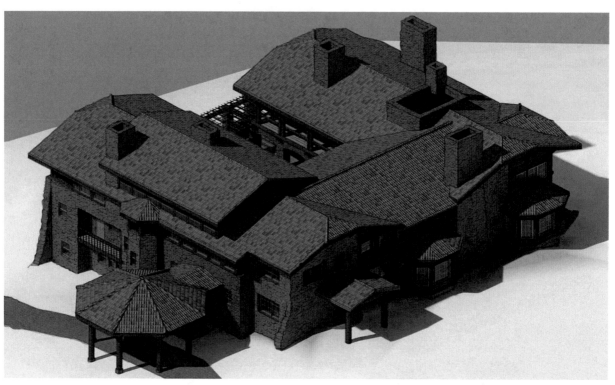

Northwest aerial views

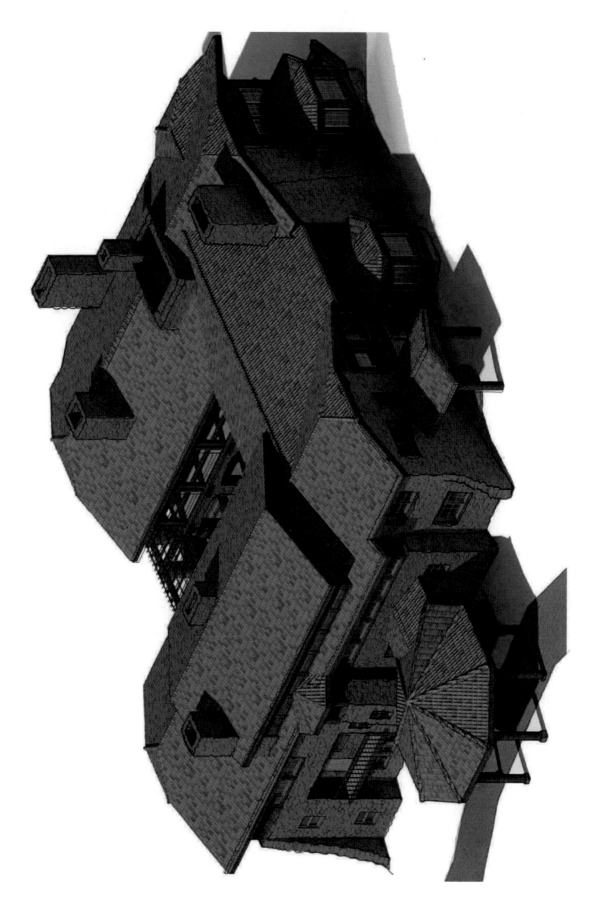

Northeast aerial view

East entry from Hill Road; view based on photograph taken with horses and wagon in foreground.

South elevation

Credits

Cover photograph and other images on pages 15 (bottom), 16 (bottom), 17 (bottom), 20, 21 (top), 34–36, 37 (top), 39–40, 43 (middle and bottom), and 44 (bottom) are the copyrighted images of the Valley of the Moon Natural History Association.

Drawings and images on pages 2, 10, 11, 19, and 25 are used courtesy of California State Parks, Jack London State Historic Park (2010). Permission to duplicate the Wolf House blueprints and elevations was also granted courtesy of California State Parks for the images on pages 46–52. The Zena Holman letter on page 37 is from the state park's Holman Collection.

Photographs on pages 6–8, 11, 12 (bottom), 14, 15 (top), 16 (top), 18 (top), 21 (bottom), 28–31, 33, 41, 42, 43 (top), and 44 (top) are used courtesy of California State Parks, Jack London State Historic Park (2010).

Letters on page 12 to George Sterling, Roland Phillips, Charmian London, and Frank Scott; two letters to George Brett on page 13; from Eliza Shepard on page 16; to Joan London and the National Union Fire Insurance Company on page 35; to George Brett, Albert Farr, and Eliza [London Shepard] dated 11–26–1913 on page 36; and to N. Clark & Sons on page 37 are used with permission of the Stanford University Press.

Photographs on page 13 and top of page 17 are used with permission of Homer Haughey and Connie Johnson.

Charmian K. London's diary entries on pages 6 and 7 are used with the permission of the Henry E. Huntington Library, San Marino, California, as are the photographs on pages 12 (top), 32, 37 (bottom), and 38, and the two undated notes from Jack London to Eliza [London Shepard] on page 36.

Steven Chais' computer-generated illustrations are used with his permission: pages 3, 9, 21 (top), 22, 23, 26, 27, 46–58.

Albert Farr's sketch of the Benbow Inn on page 18 is used with the permission of the Benbow Hotel & Resort.

The newspaper articles on pages 32–34 are used with the permission of _The Press Democrat, Santa Rosa_.

The forensic report on pages 38–41 is used with permission of Dr. Robert Anderson.

The Wolf House architectural significance on page 42 is used with the permission of Sonoma State University, Anthropological Studies Center.

Illustration on page 45 is used with permission of the artist, Allison Bollman.

9-21-2010

Bibliography

"Albert Farr Obituary." *San Francisco Chronicle*. July 13, 1947. Jack London State Historic Park Interpretive Collection Accession files no. 241-107-4, 5, and 6. Glen Ellen, CA.

Anderson, Robert N., Ph.D. *Origin of Jack London's Wolf House Fire*. Transcription of oral presentation to the Annual Jack London Birthday Banquet. Jack London Foundation, Sonoma, California. January 13, 1996.

Haughey, Homer L., and Connie Kale Johnson. *Jack London Homes Album*. Stockton, CA: Heritage Publishing, 1987.

"Jack London's Castle is to Be Rebuilt at Once." *The Press Democrat, Santa Rosa*. Sunday, August, 24, 1913. Santa Rosa, CA.

"Jack London's Home Burns." *The Press Democrat, Santa Rosa*. Saturday, August, 23, 1913. Santa Rosa, CA.

James, George Wharton. "A Study of Jack London in His Prime." *Overland Monthly*. Vol. LXVIII, no. 5. May, 1917. Oakland, CA: Star Rover House, 1987.

Kingman, Russ. *A Pictorial Biography of Jack London*. New York: Crown, 1979.

London, Charmian Kittredge. *The Book of Jack London*, *vol. II.* New York: Century, 1921.

London, Jack. *Letters from Jack London*. Ed. King Hendricks & Irving Shepard. New York: Odyssey, 1965.

_____. *The Letters of Jack London*, *3 vols.* Ed. Earle Labor, Robert C. Leitz III, and I. Milo Shepard. Stanford, CA: Stanford University Press, 1988.

_____. *The Little Lady of the Big House*. New York: Macmillan, 1916.

_____. *Revolution and Other Essays*. New York: Macmillan, 1909.

Praetzellis, Mary, Allan Bramlette, Dell Upton, Adrian Praetzellis. *Cultural Resources of Jack London State Historic Park*. Rohnert Park, CA: Sonoma State University, Anthropological Studies Center, January, 1987.

Afterword

About the authors

Having worked at Jack London State Historic Park from 1976 (London's stirring Centennial Year) through 2003, for a combined total of 44 years, retired Rangers Matt Atkinson and Greg Hayes had long been aware of the need for a historically accurate and compelling visual document dedicated entirely to Jack London's Wolf House. It was not until after they had retired from active (read "paid") park duty that they found the time and resources to put one together. Having moved on to other pursuits, both authors still spend time volunteering for the state park in Glen Ellen where Jack London threw out his anchor over a century ago.

Matt Atkinson

Greg Hayes

A publication of the

Valley of the Moon Natural History Association

Author Jack London's Sonoma Valley home, Wolf House, has fascinated visitors from all over the world since its tragic destruction in 1913. Now read about the circumstances of its rise and fall and see all of the rare photographs of the dream house collected for the first time in one book.

Visit Jack London State Historic Park online at *www.jacklondonpark.com.*

Made in the USA
Columbia, SC
06 October 2021

46819116R00038